A young person's guide to vocal health

A YOUNG PERSON'S GUIDE TO

VOCAL HEALTH

OLIVIA SPARKHALL

WITH ILLUSTRATIONS BY DAVID WALSBY

compton
PUBLISHING

Editorial offices: 35 East Street, Braunton, EX33 2EA, UK

Web: www.comptonpublishing.co.uk

ISBN 978-1-909082-71-7

A catalogue record for this book is available from the British Library.
Cover design: Mojo Creative Studio Limited, https://www.mojostudio.co.uk

To my husband, Christopher, and son, Thomas.

Contents

Acknowledgements

In acknowledgement of all the voice experts whose research has taught me so much; we stand on the shoulders of giants. To Noel McPherson at Compton Publishing for taking on this book without hesitation, for his advice, and for his vision in the My Voice Matters series. To the team at Voice Study Centre and, in particular, Debbie Winter, for her support and encouragement as I have developed and honed my expertise in the voice. To Jenevora Williams for so generously providing feedback and suggestions, and for being such an inspiration in this field. To my students at Godolphin School, Salisbury, especially the members of Godolphin Vocal Ensemble, for their astute comments and invaluable advice. To my father, David Walsby, for the care and attention he lavished on the technical drawings and illustrations.

Olivia Sparkhall, April 2022

Foreword

I am thrilled that Olivia Sparkhall has created such a valuable resource for young people. Having a voice is fundamental to our identity, expression, and communication; if the health of our voice is compromised, our identity is also affected.

For young people, who are finding their voice in the world, this is an essential read. The book presents a balanced view on use and abuse of the voice, it dispels some myths and gives easy to follow practical advice. Health and wellbeing is a complex interaction of the mind, the body and the environment; all of these aspects are illustrated here, against the background of growth, change and development.

A Young Person's Guide to Vocal Health is immensely practical, relevant and well-researched. This is an essential resource for those who sing and act as well as their teachers.

Jenevora Williams, PhD
Singing Teacher and Voice Rehabilitation specialist, and author of *Teaching Singing to Children and Young Adults* 2nd Edition.

Introduction

Your voice matters. Of course it does. You want to be able to speak and sing, clearly and freely. But how much do you actually know about your voice and how to keep it working well for you? This book aims to answer all of your questions, even the ones you hadn't thought to ask!

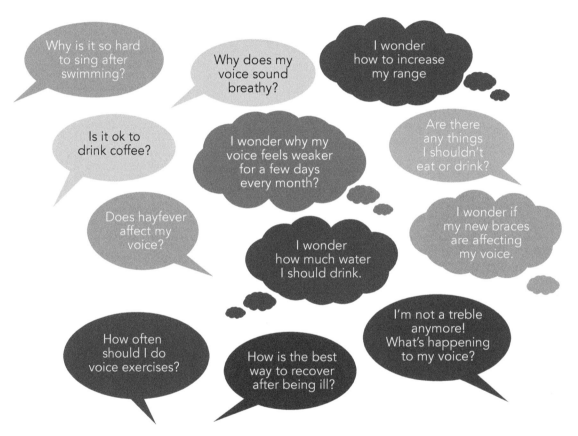

As your voice is part of your body, things which might seem unrelated to your voice can affect your vocal health. Each of the sections in this book covers a different aspect of voice health and, within each, key words or terms are colour-coded as follows:

Colour key

Anatomy/muscles - violet
Hormones - indigo
Water - blue
Cool down - light blue
Healthy - green

Unhealthy - brown
Warm up - orange
Very important - red
Recovery - dark red
Breathing - grey

In addition to the colour coding, you'll find sticky notes to inform and help you.

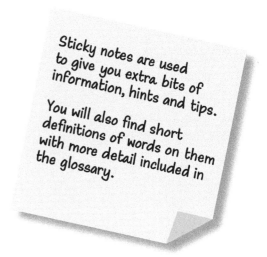

Sticky notes are used to give you extra bits of information, hints and tips.

You will also find short definitions of words on them with more detail included in the glossary.

My aim is to help you to keep a healthy voice and to explain what is going on when your voice seems to have gone wrong. There is a reading list (books and websites) at the back so that you can explore things further if you wish.

My Voice Matters Flowchart

Your roadmap to good vocal health

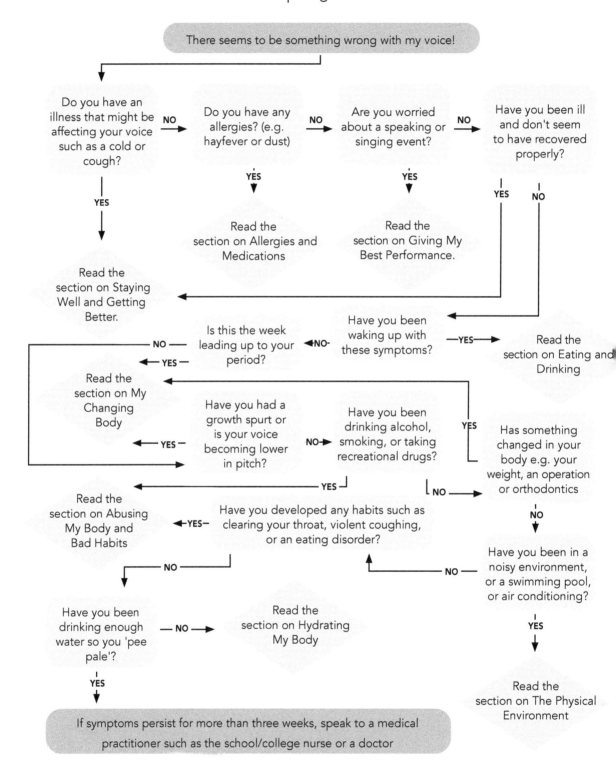

There seems to be something wrong with my voice!

Do you have an illness that might be affecting your voice such as a cold or cough? — NO → Do you have any allergies? (e.g. hayfever or dust) — NO → Are you worried about a speaking or singing event? — NO → Have you been ill and don't seem to have recovered properly?

YES (allergies) → Read the section on Allergies and Medications

YES (worried) → Read the section on Giving My Best Performance.

YES (illness) → Read the section on Staying Well and Getting Better.

Have you been ill and don't seem to have recovered properly? — YES / NO

Have you been waking up with these symptoms? — YES → Read the section on Eating and Drinking

NO → Is this the week leading up to your period? — NO → Read the section on My Changing Body / YES →

Have you had a growth spurt or is your voice becoming lower in pitch? — YES →

Have you been drinking alcohol, smoking, or taking recreational drugs? — NO → / YES →

Has something changed in your body e.g. your weight, an operation or orthodontics — YES / NO

Read the section on Abusing My Body and Bad Habits

Have you developed any habits such as clearing your throat, violent coughing, or an eating disorder? — YES → Read the section on Abusing My Body and Bad Habits

NO →

Have you been drinking enough water so you 'pee pale'? — NO → Read the section on Hydrating My Body

YES →

Have you been in a noisy environment, or a swimming pool, or air conditioning? — YES → Read the section on The Physical Environment

NO →

If symptoms persist for more than three weeks, speak to a medical practitioner such as the school/college nurse or a doctor

1 What is my voice and how does it work?

♫ **making a sound**

♫ **anatomy**

♫ **function**

Making a sound

When your vocal folds vibrate together you make a sound. Air has to move between the folds to make this happen, and this almost always takes place on an exhalation. The sounds you make are shaped in the vocal tract (the area between your larynx and your lips) using muscles including your tongue (which is also a muscle).

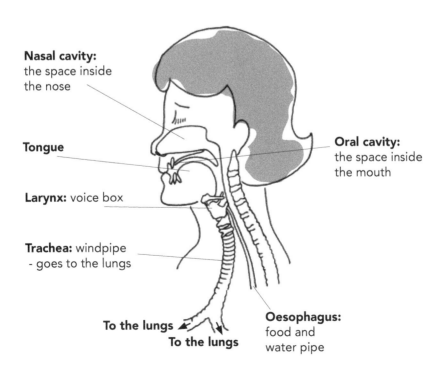

Nasal cavity: the space inside the nose

Tongue

Larynx: voice box

Trachea: windpipe - goes to the lungs

Oral cavity: the space inside the mouth

To the lungs

To the lungs

Oesophagus: food and water pipe

Anatomy

We can take a closer look at the larynx to see how it works.

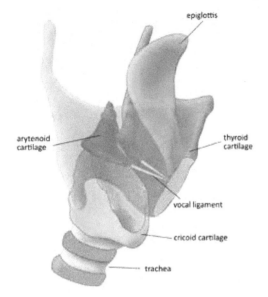

The epiglottis covers up the trachea (tube down to the lungs) when you are eating or drinking to stop food and drink going down the wrong way.

The cartilages move to help you change voice register (when you go from low voice to high voice).

The cartilages also form an protective cage around the delicate vocal folds.

The side view of the Larynx.
Image courtesy *A Singer's Guide to the Larynx*.

Now let us have a look inside from the back to the front.
Remember you are standing behind a person, looking at their neck.
Imagine someone has removed their spine.

The vocal folds open and close very quickly to create a sound. They rely on air being pushed up from below to do this effectively.

The whole area around the vocal folds (the mucosal membranes) needs to be moist like the inside of your mouth in order to work well.

Lubricating fluid is produced in the false folds.

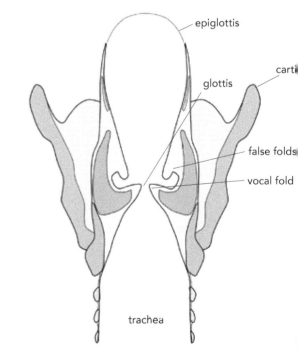

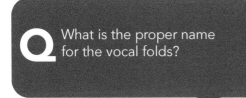

Q What is the proper name for the vocal folds?

A Vocal folds is probably the best description, but you might hear them called 'vocal cords' or 'vocal chords' because they look a bit like string.

Finally, we are going to chop someone's head off and look down their neck at their vocal folds. We are standing in front of this person.

Glottis viewed from above – folds open

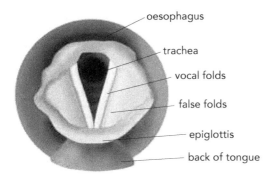

oesophagus

trachea

vocal folds

false folds

epiglottis

back of tongue

Glottis viewed from above – folds closed

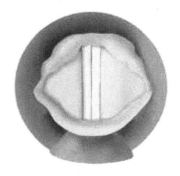

In the left hand image above, the vocal folds are open and the person is breathing normally.

In the right hand image, the vocal folds are touching. The person may be speaking or singing.

3

2 Before and after I use my voice

 morning warm-up routine

 breathing exercises

 voice exercises

 singing healthily

 cool downs

Warming up

Warming up the voice is a very good idea even if you do not plan to sing. Here is a morning warm-up that can be done in the shower or your room. You can also use it before any singing you do during the day. Before you start, make sure you have had a glass of water to drink and check you are not going to hit anything when you stretch.

muscles	breath	sound	range
• Roll your shoulders back and forwards. • Give each leg a shake. • Reach up to the ceiling with both arms and slowly lower them.	• Exhale to 'shhhhh' until you run out of breath. • Repeat with 'sssss', and 'fffff'.	• Do some low-pitched lip trills 'brrrrrr'* making a rumbling sound. • Repeat with mid-pitch, and high-pitch.	• Make some sounds getting higher each time: 'mmm' (think 'it's yummy') 'whoo' (like a ghost) • Belly laughs 'he, he, he'.

*try to make your lips vibrate 'brrrrr' for as long as you can.

Some people will need to press in and up gently, pointing towards the tip of the nose, just above the corner of their mouth. This will release tight muscles so their lips can buzz freely.

Did you know?

Doing long high-pitched lip trills 'brrr' can help to extend your upper range.

Breathing Exercises

Regular breathing practice can help you to be able to sing longer phrases in one breath and to have a wider range of dynamics (louds and softs). It is also a brilliant way to calm nerves and aid relaxation. You can do this exercise silently, or exhale to 'shhhh', 'sssss' or 'fffff'.

| Breathe in deeply as you count to 3 | → | Exhale slowly as you count to 6 | → | Breathe in deeply as you count to 4 | → | Exhale slowly as you count to 8 |

- Keep arms and shoulders relaxed.
- Try breathing in with your hands on your head.

- Feel your abdominal (tummy) muscles tighten at the end of the exhalation.

- Feel the air making your abdomen (tummy) expand.

- The aim of this exercise is to gradually lengthen the exhalation. Try exhaling to 10 counts.

Think about where you are doing your breathing exercises. Some people are affected by breathing in the scent from air fresheners or by dusty environments. Sometimes air-conditioned or centrally heated rooms can be very drying.

Try this exercise in the bathroom if you need a more humid place!

Voice Exercises

There are lots of **voice exercises** which help you to develop your singing technique including tongue twisters, jaw release, blowing bubbles through a straw, nasal sounds, different onsets, creating resonance, and vowel sounds. Daily practice will help you to develop a strong, confident singing voice. There is a list of recommended books and websites at the back of this book with some more voice exercises. Here are some to try now:

'Puffy cheeks'
This is a really gentle exercise that can help with voice recovery after illness.

- Put your finger on your closed lips
- Breathe in through your nose
- Keeping your lips closed, fill up your cheeks with air
- Allow a tiny space to form around your finger as you…
- …slide up and down a five-note scale
- It might sound ghostly 'whoo' or like a revving car
  - ✓ Your finger should feel warm
  - ✓ You should feel and hear air escaping

'Silent in-breath'
This is to help you make sure your vocal folds are fully open when you breathe in before singing. Starting to sing like this is called 'smooth onset' singing.

- Gently breathe in through your nose
- And out through your mouth
- Notice that both the inhalation and exhalation were silent
- Now breathe in through your mouth
- And out through your mouth noticing that both in and out is still silent
- Now breathe in through your mouth and pause…
- Before breathing out through your mouth
  - ✓ Your vocal folds should stay open throughout
  - ✓ You should notice the 'open' feeling in your throat
- Finally try singing a long note, or some short notes on the exhalation
  - ✓ Notice the vocal folds interrupting the breath flow
  - ✓ Notice you can now make the exhalation longer

This is what fully open vocal folds look like.

'Vowel sounds'

Each vowel sound is made in a different part of the mouth. Try saying the vowels 'a, e, i, o, u' (ay, ee, eye, oh, ooh) and notice how your mouth shape, tongue, and lips move to a different position for each sound.

You can explore this further by playing with the pink trombone model. Go to https://imaginary.org/program/pink-trombone and click launch. Use the mouse, or your finger, to change the shape of the tongue, mouth, lip and throat and try changing the pitch and the onset.

- Gently breathe in through your mouth
- Close your lips and hum 'mmm' on a comfortable, but quite low pitch
- Breathe in again and alternate between 'mmm' and 'may' – 'mmm, may, mmm, may'
- Repeat with 'me', 'my', 'mo' and 'moo'
  - ✓ Notice how your tongue changes position when the vowel sound changes
  - ✓ Notice how your lips change position when the vowel sound changes
- Now try the same exercise at a higher pitch.

Singing healthily

Singing healthily means:

- being well-hydrated
- having a healthy vocal tract (neck, throat, mouth and nose)
- developing a technique that avoids unnecessary tension or stress
- avoiding activities or habits that are damaging
- not limiting your range or style during voice change

This book covers each of these areas in more detail.

Cooling down

Cooling down after singing resets your voice by bringing your larynx (voice box) back to a relaxed state and allowing muscles to release (lengthen). Follow these steps to make sure your voice is ready for tomorrow:

Reposition your larynx (voice box) → **Lengthen your muscles** → **Release any tension**

- Lip trill 'brrr' down to your lowest notes.
- Vocalise 'meee' down to your lowest notes.
- Hum 'mmm' down to your lowest notes.

- Stretch arms above head and slowly lower them.
- Roll shoulders backwards and forwards.
- Flop down so your head is near your knees; slowly unwind.

- Massage your throat, neck and jaw muscles (see page 18).
- Follow the steps in the Staying Well and Getting Better chapter.
- Have a good night's sleep!

If you can, one of the best ways to unwind is to lie down in the 'semi-supine' position. This is lying on your back with your knees bent and your feet by your bottom.

Try taking some deep breaths in this position and feel the muscles in your back pressing into the floor when you inhale.

Always get up slowly!

3 Hydrating my body

 The No.1 most important thing you can do to keep your voice healthy is to drink enough water.

If you are dehydrated you are...

more likely to get ill

going to find it harder to sing

more likely to develop voice problems

If you are dehydrated you will find it harder to produce your best voice.

Hydrated is your body having enough water to function well.

Dehydrated means there is not enough water in your body for it to function well.

Rehydrate is when you drink enough to allow your body to function at its best.

For your brain to function well it is important to be well hydrated.

11

When, what and how much to drink

You need to rehydrate after sleeping, so morning drinking is key:

- Have **at least** 500 ml of water soon after waking
- Finish **another** 500 ml of water before the end of your first lesson (or at break)
- Drink **a further** 500 ml of water before lunchtime
- In the afternoon, drink **at least an additional** 500 ml of water

Most recent research on this topic says that school children should drink a minimum of 2 litres a day. Singers and those doing a lot of speaking will need to drink **more**, as will anyone who takes part in sports activities. In order to achieve this, you will need to carry a **water bottle** with you and know how much water it holds by either looking at the label or using a measuring jug to find out.

> **500 + 500 + 500 + 500 = 2 litres;
> the minimum you should drink each day.**

Q How do I know I have been drinking enough?

A Pee pale!

Q What is that?

A Wee that does not smell and is almost clear in colour.

Q But my wee is green!

A This might be medication, vitamin supplements, food colouring or asparagus (which also makes it smell funny!)

'Pee pale' is good advice but is not always completely reliable. Other indicators to your needing to drink more are: feeling thirsty, having a headache, and feeling dizzy or faint.

You will need to drink more if

♪ you are in a rehearsal (singing or speaking)

♪ you are exercising

♪ the weather is hot

♪ you are in an air-conditioned environment

♪ you have been swimming

Drinking during a rehearsal

- washes away irritants
- moistens dry throats (from mouth breathing)
- helps mucosal membranes* repel bacteria
- makes sure you are hydrated for tomorrow

Carry me with you and refill me throughout the day.

Wash me regularly and reuse me – great for the environment!

Your mucosal membranes (*cells around your vocal folds) need to be plumped up. This only happens if your body has plenty of processed fluid available.

You can think of this as:

today's drinking = tomorrow's hydration

Is it ok to drink coffee?

Are there any things I shouldn't eat or drink?

Does hayfever affect my voice?

How is the best way to recover after being ill?

4 Staying well and getting better

♫ Staying healthy
♫ **A good recovery**
♫ **Steam or nebuliser?**
♫ **Releasing muscle tension**

Staying healthy

The **four key elements** to staying healthy form a virtuous circle:

You must be sure to drink enough water (see Chapter 3 **Hydrating my body**)

You can also **avoid catching a cold or cough** by

- regularly washing your hands
- avoiding touching your face
- avoiding crowded environments
- thoroughly washing shared items such as mugs and cutlery
- not sharing items such as water bottles and toiletries

A good recovery

Here is what to do if you become ill:

✔ stop exercising
✔ stay warm
✔ increase fluid intake (more than 2 litres a day)
✔ gentle vocal warm-ups (see warming up)
✖ do not sing if it hurts or if you cannot make sound

good
diet

enough
sleep

avoid
stress

regular
exercise

Removing exercise from the virtuous circle helps your body to focus on recovering.

Steam or nebuliser?

You may have heard that breathing in steam or the vapour produced by a nebuliser can aid recovery. Unless you are old enough to cope carefully, this should only be done under the supervision of an adult so please speak to a parent/guardian or the school/college nurse and they will help you.

There are four options (always take great care with hot water):

- Head over a bowl of steaming water with a towel over your head
- A hand-held inhaler filled with steaming water
- An electronic steam inhaler
- A nebuliser with isotonic saline (0.9% sodium chloride solution)*

*Current research rates this option the highest.

Do not add anything to the water (no menthol, eucalyptus, essential oils etc.) and remember that everything you use should be washed thoroughly (and nebuliser equipment must be sterilised - be sure to follow the instructions). All equipment should be cleaned thoroughly before anyone else uses it.

After steaming, **wait half an hour** before singing.

Head over a bowl of water
Use the towel to trap the steam and take long, slow breaths.

A hand-held inhaler
Fill with very hot water and inhale the steam.

A nebuliser with 0.9% saline
Use a nose-and-mouth mask (pictured) or just a mouth tube.

Warning! Take care when handling hot water!

A warm, steamy bath can also be a great way to relax, releasing tense muscles and helping you to de-stress.

Releasing muscle tension

The muscles in your neck and throat can become tense and 'forget' how to relax. This can happen if you have been ill with a cough, or if you have been singing when you have not been well. It can also happen if you have been stressed or nervous. You can massage your jaw, throat and neck to help relieve muscle tension. This is also part of the cool down routine explained on page 10.

You might like to use massage oil or body moisturiser when you carry out self-massage.

First of all, have a good stretch and roll your shoulders like in the cool downs.

Then…

Find your jaw-bone under your ears with your fingers

Gently massage the area under your jaw-bone from behind your ears down and inwards to your chin.

Find the muscles that run down the side of your neck

Using circular motion with your fingertips, massage from behind your ears down to your shoulders.

With the fingertip and thumb-tip of one hand, find either side of your larynx (voice box)

Very gently massage from under your jaw-bone down to your collar-bone.

- Be gentle
- Just use fingertips
- If an area is tender, use circular motions to release tension
- If it hurts, stop.

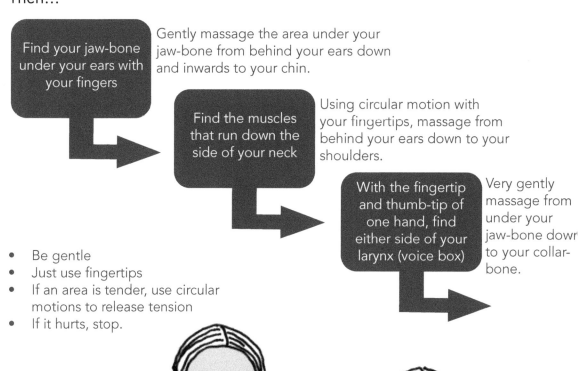

5 Allergies & medications

 **Allergies**

♫ **Medications and alternative medication**

♫ **Asthma**

Allergies

Even when symptoms are mild, allergies can affect your voice. The best thing to do to treat these symptoms is to rinse out your nose. This removes the particles causing the allergic inflammation.

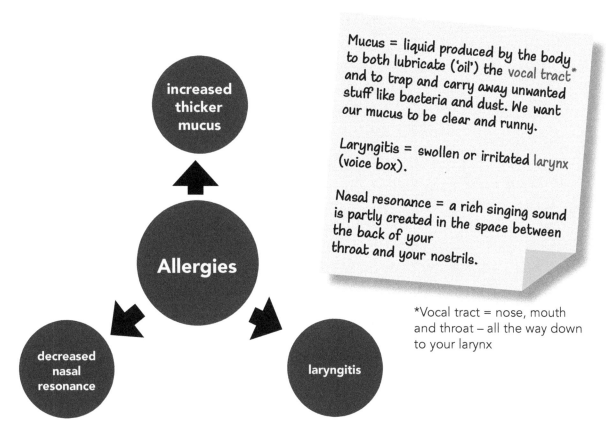

increased thicker mucus

Allergies

decreased nasal resonance

laryngitis

Mucus = liquid produced by the body to both lubricate ('oil') the vocal tract* and to trap and carry away unwanted stuff like bacteria and dust. We want our mucus to be clear and runny.

Laryngitis = swollen or irritated larynx (voice box).

Nasal resonance = a rich singing sound is partly created in the space between the back of your throat and your nostrils.

*Vocal tract = nose, mouth and throat – all the way down to your larynx

19

Treat with a sinus rinse, a neti pot or a prescription nasal spray.

Using a neti pot

Using a sinus rinse

Medications

It is very important to seek advice from your doctor or pharmacist on any medication you take because some medications can cause dryness and make your voice worse. There is usually an alternative, but you must mention to the doctor, nurse or pharmacist that you are a singer/actor who needs to avoid drying out your vocal tract. This includes the contraceptive pill, and medication for reflux, anxiety, depression, acne, and asthma inhalers. CONTINUE to take your medication but speak to a medical professional if you think it might be causing dryness, hoarseness or affecting the sound your voice makes.

> Remember to mention to your doctor or pharmacist that you are a singer before you start any new medication. There are often alternatives available which can avoid affecting your singing.

Asthma

Asthma causes a narrowing of the airways. This will affect your breath control (how long you can sing for without needing to breathe in) and your lung capacity (how much air you can breathe in). You may also have developed unhelpful muscle tension or strain. Doing the breathing exercises on page 7 will help to maximise your lung capacity. The massage techniques on page 18 will help to relieve muscle tension caused by asthma. If you are an asthmatic it is very important to follow the advice of your doctor and take your prevention inhaler. You should follow the instructions you have been given.

> Using a spacer with your inhaler is a good idea because it allows you to inhale more slowly and more deeply.

6 Giving my best performance

Performance anxiety, stage fright, butterflies in the stomach, feeling nervous are all the same thing: they are the natural response of the body before a performance. It is really important to take the symptoms seriously and to practise being in control of them as you develop into a confident performer. This can take time to achieve.

The body's release of adrenalin (the chemical that makes you feel nervous) can result in any (or none!) of the following symptoms:

- Sweating
- Shaking
- Heart beating fast
- Very tense muscles
- Extra saliva
- Shallow breathing
- Problems swallowing
- Dry mouth

If the symptoms are too severe, they can make the performance go badly. However, many people find that the extra focus created by adrenalin flowing around the body helps the performance to go really well.

Understanding the stress response:
- Read one of the recommended resources on page 42
- Practise the breathing exercises on page 7
- Use the self-massage techniques on page 18
- Speak to a medical practitioner e.g. a school nurse
- See a professional counsellor

Remember – you must ask for help if you are struggling.

21

Here is some advice from other young performers like you:

Remember that the audience wants you to do well and is supporting you not judging you. (GCSE student)

Practise singing your piece in front of a smaller group of people such as your family or friends. (aged 16)

Find a quiet place beforehand to compose yourself, and then talking to yourself, reassuring yourself, is often a good way to help. (aged 15)

I always find it is helpful to breathe deeply and to shake out my hands. (aged 12)

I find that taking ten deep breaths and going on stage with a smile helps me a lot. (aged 11)

7 Eating and drinking

 What, and what not to eat and drink

 Reflux

Diet plays an important part in maintaining good health. You should eat a wide variety of foods that are low in fat and sugar, and high in carbohydrates and fibre. There are also specific vitamins and minerals that help the body to stay healthy.

Troublesome foods to eat just before singing, are foods that cause the claggy feeling of mucus hanging around in the nose and throat for a bit. The list is quite long because these foods vary from person to person and include things like dairy products, chocolate, nuts, fizzy drinks and orange juice.

Some people are not affected so use a food diary if you want to find out which (if any) cause the feeling of thick mucus for you.

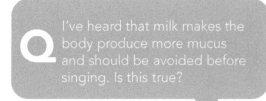

I've heard that milk makes the body produce more mucus and should be avoided before singing. Is this true?

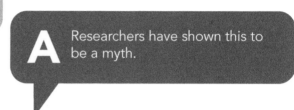

Researchers have shown this to be a myth.

Reflux

Sometimes stomach acid can come up your oesophagus (food pipe) and irritate your larynx (voice box) or throat. The symptoms may include:

- bad (smelly) breath
- needing longer to warm up
- the sensation of a lump in the throat
- a sore throat for a long time
- a cough for a long time
- hoarseness

This is known as reflux, or acid reflux.

For some people, some foods might make this worse. These include acidic foods: tomato products, pizza, acidic fruits. Also: soft drinks, chocolate, fatty foods, spicy foods and onions.

If you think you might be affected by this, you should speak to a medical practitioner. As said above, the best way of finding out which foods affect you is to keep a food diary. Also, try not to eat a meal and then go straight to bed. When you do lie down, lying on your left side helps reduce reflux because this positions your stomach below your oesophagus (food pipe) and helps to stop acids returning to your throat.

Drinks which contain caffeine include coffee, tea, cola, and energy drinks. Caffeine makes your bladder muscle tell your brain you need to go to the toilet more often. It also relaxes the muscle that controls connection to the oesophagus so can also cause reflux.

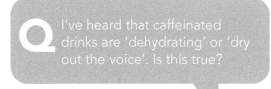

Q I've heard that caffeinated drinks are 'dehydrating' or 'dry out the voice'. Is this true?

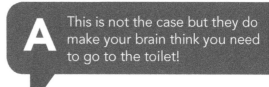

A This is not the case but they do make your brain think you need to go to the toilet!

I wonder if my new braces are affecting my voice.

I wonder why my voice feels weaker for a few days every month?

I'm not a treble anymore! What's happening to my voice?

Why is it so hard to sing after swimming?

Why does my voice sound breathy?

8 My changing body

 **Braces and operations**

♫ Growing bodies; growing voices

♫ Voice change

♫ **How hormones affect the voice**

Whose voice is affected by hormones? Everyone's! As boys and girls develop from children into adults, hormones affect how their voice changes. Voice-change might be more obvious in boys, but girls' voices change too. This section refers to typical girls and boys but not everyone fits neatly into those categories. If you would like to find out more, please see the recommended books and websites at the back of the book.

Braces and operations

Having braces fitted to your teeth can affect your speaking and singing. It can also result in unhelpful muscle tension, so massage is recommended (see page 18).

It is actually quite common to need an operation during your teenage years. For example, sometimes it is necessary to have a tooth removed or you might develop appendicitis and need to have your appendix removed.

If you need to have an operation remember to mention to your anaesthetist that you are a singer. This can affect what sort of intubation is used, and how it is inserted.

Singers should speak to their doctor about whether intubation (a tube put down your windpipe to help you breathe) is necessary and whether a laryngeal mask can be used instead. This method can avoid the risk of damage to the vocal folds.

If you have an operation in your vocal tract (mouth, nose, throat, neck) you might need some help with vocal recovery. For example, if you have your tonsils removed, you might need some exercises to strengthen the area at the back of your throat.

Growing bodies; growing voices

As your body grows from child to adult, your voice grows too. The larynx (voice box) changes in size and shape. The vocal folds become longer and the muscles around it grow too. Understanding this can help you to figure out what is going on as you speak and sing your way through your teenage years.

Voice change

During voice-change in both boys and girls, it can be hard to control the voice for a while. The range (number of notes you can sing) might become narrower for a bit, and the voice quality (how the voice sounds) will also change.

Boys and girls develop differently…

A girl's larynx (voice box) grows by about 34%. Sometimes the changes in girls' voices are not as obvious as those in boys'. Experiments show that between early teens (Year 7) and late teens (Year 12), teenage girls singing voices improve in tuning, control of onset (the start of the note), pitch control of sung consonants (the ends of notes), and the development of vibrato.

As a boy's voice changes the most recent advice is for him to start speaking and singing in his new voice (but it is fine for him to keep using his treble (high) singing voice too). A boy's larynx (voice box) grows by about 65% and changes shape. That is why it is possible to see the larynxes of some men sticking out of their neck (their 'Adam's apple').

…but they can both experience similar issues during voice-change throughout their teenage years. The box below lists some of them:

- Lack of control over pitch
- Voice cracking when singing
- Noticeable changes between registers (low singing voice and high singing voice)
- Difficulty producing sound (may be uncomfortable)
- Hoarseness
- Temporarily husky-sounding
- Temporary smaller range (can't sing so high or so low for now)
- Voice sounds breathy (can hear extra air in the sung notes)

and speaking voice lowers in pitch

You should continue to do the gentle warm-ups and gentle exercises on pages 5 and 8 as this will help your larynx (voice box) to remain flexible as your voice develops.

How hormones affect the voice

Girls need to know that hormone changes during the week before their period comes can also affect their voice. This is normal (90% of women experience some PMS symptoms during this time each month) and can be really mild and not noticeable.

If you are experiencing symptoms you should check your diary or, if you have one, your tracker app.

Did you know?
PMS stands for Pre-Menstrual Syndrome. There are a lot of PMS symptoms which you can find out about in the further reading at the end.

Do you use an app to track your periods? It can be a really helpful way of keeping an eye on your cycle and noticing patterns. There are lots of free ones available — just search 'period tracker' in your phone's app store.

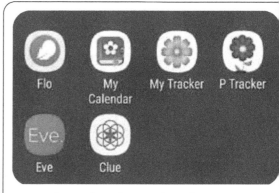

Examples of period tracker apps

The box below contains examples of how PMS may affect your voice:

- Voice is weaker than normal
- Tuning might be affected
- Voice feels tired, or gets tired quickly
- Range is narrower (fewer notes)
- Voice is slightly hoarse

- Slightly lower speaking voice
- Voice might sound different
- Harder to sing fast notes
- Mucus is thicker
- Harder to sing quiet high notes

Remember – you may only experience one of these changes, and it may only last a day. Some people do not notice any changes at all.

9 Abusing my body and bad habits

♫ Singing safely and not overdoing it

♫ Bad habits

♫ Physical alignment

♫ Eating disorders

♫ Alcohol

♫ Smoking and drugs (the illegal kind)

Singing safely and not overdoing it

Your body is your instrument, so you need to take care of your whole body (physical and mental) to have a healthy voice. When you sing, your vocal folds meet and part hundreds of times a second and lots of muscles work together to achieve a precise result. Your vocal folds and muscles benefit from recovery time so it is important to rest.

This might mean not talking during the breaks in rehearsals or when travelling to and from the performance venue. Singing for a long time without a break can be tiring and may result in temporary hoarseness. If you have a whole day of rehearsals it is a good idea to pace yourself. You should certainly do the cool downs recommended on page 10 after a day of singing.

Bad habits

Bad habits that continue for a long time can damage the vocal folds. You should try to avoid clearing your throat and coughing violently.

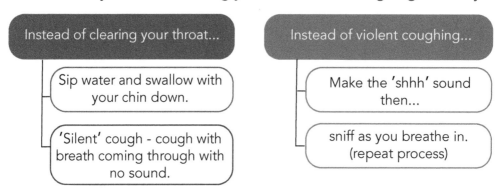

Instead of clearing your throat...
- Sip water and swallow with your chin down.
- 'Silent' cough - cough with breath coming through with no sound.

Instead of violent coughing...
- Make the 'shhh' sound then...
- sniff as you breathe in. (repeat process)

Physical alignment

When standing and sitting, it is really easy to get into bad habits which can affect your voice. For instance, crossing your legs, jutting out your chin, slumping your shoulders, standing on one leg, or leaning forward - all of these habits can affect breathing and sound production. Taking Alexander Technique lessons is one way of helping you to unlearn bad habits and realign your body.

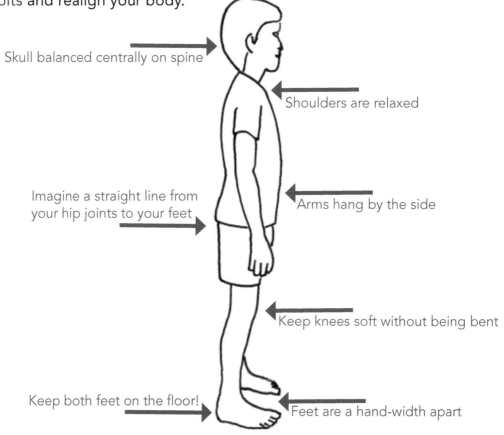

Skull balanced centrally on spine

Shoulders are relaxed

Imagine a straight line from your hip joints to your feet

Arms hang by the side

Keep knees soft without being bent

Keep both feet on the floor!

Feet are a hand-width apart

Eating disorders

If you think you might be suffering from an eating disorder* you should try and get help as soon as you can. **Please talk to the school nurse, or any other medical practitioner, or adult at school or college. Many people are here to support you.**

Bulimia (being sick after meals on purpose) can cause hoarseness, a painful larynx (voice box), make your body produce more mucus, make you lose your voice for a short time, and make your voice lower in pitch.

Anorexia can affect how powerful your voice is and make it harder to produce sound.

Advice from teenagers who have had eating disorders is to 'seek help as soon as possible, even if it feels hard to talk about it'.

*using food to try and manage your feelings.

Alcohol

Alcohol can

- make reflux worse (see page 24)
- dehydrate the body and the mucosal membranes around the vocal folds (see page 11)
- numb the larynx (voice box) leading to damage caused by unhealthy singing
- lead to damage caused by over-singing or singing with poor technique

Singing after having had an alcoholic drink can affect

- muscle coordination
- concentration
- focus
- memory
- self-perception

You should not drink alcohol…

- and then sing
- and expect to be able to sing well the following day

Smoking and drugs

Smoking (tobacco and cannabis) can damage your voice beyond repair. It...

- irritates the respiratory tract (the breathing tube and lungs)
- causes long-term damage to the vocal folds

The results of smoking are
- inflamed (swollen) vocal folds
- chronic structural changes (changing the vocal tract forever)
- throat cancer

Smoking tobacco	Smoking cannabis	Vaping
• sticks tar and other irritants directly onto the vocal folds. • permanently changes the cells of the vocal folds.	• burns at really high temperatures. • has an even worse effect on the tissues of the larynx, changing how clear the notes sound (sometimes forever).	• harms the surface of the lungs. • deposits toxic chemicals onto the vocal folds.

Just being in a smoky atmosphere (even if you are not smoking yourself) can

- Cause problems with your sinuses
- Cause problems with the lining of your nose
- Make asthma worse
- Affect your breathing

Cocaine increases blood flow to the vocal folds causing them to swell and affecting vocal quality (the sound the voice makes).

You risk your vocal health if you take illegal drugs.

10 The physical environment

♫ **Raising your voice in a lot of background noise (the Lombard effect)**

♫ **Yelling and screaming**

♫ **The physical nature of the environment**

♫ **Swimming pools**

The Lombard effect

Talking where there is a lot of background noise can be really tiring on the voice and affect vocal health. You should take care in noisy places like dining rooms and canteens, at concerts and sports matches in stadiums and sports halls, and in rooms where there are lot of other people talking at the same time. Speaking and singing in noisy environments is bad for vocal health, particularly when the voice is already tired. You might strain the muscles of the larynx (voice box) or cause the vocal folds to swell. The reason for this is something called the Lombard effect. *This is where you raise your voice and speak differently when there is background noise so that you can hear yourself speak and be heard by others.*

Yelling and screaming

You should take great care not to yell. When playing sport, it is best to remain silent when running, jumping, kicking or catching. If you need to shout you should stand still to avoid vocal damage. Very noisy environments where there is yelling or screaming can lead to permanently damaged hearing. For example, exposure to 106 decibels (noise of a leaf blower) should not exceed 3.75 minutes a day without ear protection.

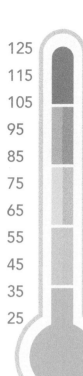

125	- Dangerously loud gunshot
115	- Fire alarm
105	- Pneumatic drill
95	- Hair dryer
85	- Maximum safe limit*
75	- Vacuum cleaner
65	- Normal conversation
55	- Rainfall
45	- Refrigerator hum
35	- Rustling leaves
25	- Breathing

A decibel meter (or 'sound meter') measures how loud something is in decibels (dB)

*Any sound above 85dB can damage your hearing. You should limit your daily exposure to loud sounds.

If you are concerned about a particular environment, you should borrow a decibel meter, or download a decibel meter app, to see if the environment is too loud.

Many people use earplugs to protect their ears. You may have seen that the children of celebrities often wear ear defenders in loud environments such as theatres, football matches and pop concerts. This is because they know how dangerously loud these events can be. Hearing loss can be catastrophic to a singer and end their performing career.

The physical nature of the environment

This can also have a bad effect on vocal health.

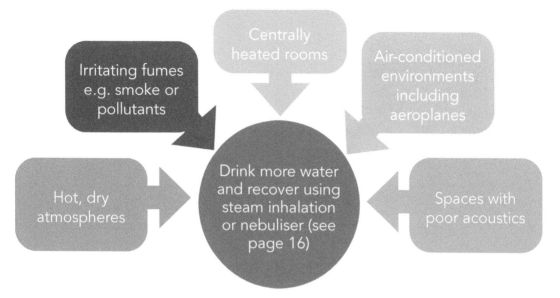

All of these can affect how your voice works, causing the mucus-producing cells to produce too much or too little mucus.

Swimming pools

Swimmers beware!

- breathing through the mouth causes the vocal tract to dry out
- breathing in chlorinated air (the air just above the surface of the water) irritates the mucosal membranes (see page 11)

Cheering on team-members at galas can result in hoarseness because the noise rebounds off the hard surfaces meaning the supporters have to cheer louder and louder in order to make themselves heard.

- ✘ Not talking on the coach journey home can help to prevent additional vocal damage.
- ✔ Drink plenty of water before, during, and after swimming.
- ✔ Use a steam inhaler or nebuliser to aid voice recovery afterwards.
- ✘ Avoid swimming immediately before a singing concert.

Glossary

Abdomen is often called your tummy or stomach. It is the area below your ribs and above your pelvis.

Acoustics is the quality of sound in a space.

Adam's Apple is another word for the larynx or voice box.

Adrenalin is the chemical released in your body that makes you feel nervous.

Cartilage is a firm, rubber-like part of your body that is softer and more flexible than bone.

Decibel is the measurement for dynamics (how loud or soft; sometimes called volume).

Dehydrated means there is not enough water in your body for it to function well.

Ear, Nose & Throat (ENT) Doctor is a doctor who specialises in problems with your ears, nose and throat.

Epiglottis is a flap of cartilage which covers up the trachea to stop food and drink going down the 'wrong way'.

Exhalation is the out-breath.

Glottis is the space between the vocal folds.

Hoarse is when your voice sounds croaky, breathy or rough due to voice problems.

Hormones are chemicals made by your body to help it function properly.

Hydrated is your body having enough water to function well.

Inhalation is the in-breath.

Laryngologist is an ENT doctor who is an expert in voice problems.

Larynx is the voice box, sometimes called the Adam's Apple.

Laryngitis is when your larynx is irritated or swollen.

Lombard effect describes needing to raise your voice to be heard in noisy environments.

Mucosal membranes are the areas inside your vocal tract which produce a special watery fluid which keeps everything moist and lubricated.

Nebuliser is a machine which produces a special vapour of tiny droplets (much smaller than normal water droplets) a bit like a mist.

Neti pot is a little jug designed to be filled with saltwater solution and used to rinse out your nose.

Oesophagus is the scientific name for the tube which takes food and drink to your stomach.

Onset is how the sung note starts. It can be smooth, harsh or breathy.

Physical alignment refers to how the different parts of your body fit together without causing pain or excessive tension.

Pre-Menstrual Syndrome (PMS) is a phrase used to cover all of the symptoms experienced during the week before (and few days after) your period starts each month.

Rehydrate is when you drink enough to allow your body to function at its best.

Reflux is when stomach acid comes up your oesophagus and irritates your larynx or throat.

Resonance is a rich singing sound created in your vocal tract.

Respiratory Tract is the trachea and the lungs.

Sinus rinse is a squirty bottle with saltwater solution which is used to rinse out your nose.

Speech and Language Therapists (SLT) help people with speech, language and communication problems.

Trachea is the scientific name for the windpipe which carries air from your mouth/nose to your lungs.

Vocal folds are the tissues stretched across the larynx which vibrate when air passes through them to make a sound.

Vocal ligaments help to strengthen the vocal fold tissue.

Vocal tract includes the spaces inside your neck, throat, mouth and nose.

Voice Clinic is where lots of different voice-professionals work together to help people with voice problems.

Further reading
Books and websites

Before and after I use my voice

Sing! Vocal Warm-ups for all Styles by Paul Knight includes fun vocal warm-ups plus a download card which provides links to mp3 backing tracks.

This is a Voice by Jeremy Fisher and Gillyanne Kayes presents different sets of warm-ups, exercises and cool downs for different occasions and a section on the science 'how the voice works'.

If you want to find out even more about the science of the voice try *A Singer's Guide to the Larynx* by Nicola Harrison and Alan Watson which features really clear anatomical drawings and descriptions.

A guide to building your own warm-up can be found here:
https://www.voicescienceworks.org/build-your-own-warm-up.html

Here is an animated, singing larynx:
https://youtu.be/C7CpkEszksI

Hydrating my body

Several water bottles come with trackers:
Joseph Joseph Dot Hydration Tracker
Aladdin Active Hydration Tracker
Thermos Hydration Water Bottle with Meter

Staying well and getting better; allergies and medications

How to use a neti pot video:
https://www.youtube.com/watch?v= sKlpRjgriGM
Remember – your salt solution must be made from boiled water, cooled to body temperature (not water straight out of a tap). 2.5g seasalt to 250ml water.

41

Giving my best performance

Your Life, Your Way by Joseph Ciarrochi and Louise Hayes teaches ways to help you manage anxiety.

The Teen Girl's Singing Guide by Nancy Bos has a section on performance anxiety.

There is an informative piece on stage fright (performance anxiety) here: https://www.webmd.com/anxiety-panic/guide/stage-fright-performance-anxiety

Eating and drinking

How to keep a food diary, including a pdf download to fill in: https://www.bupa.co.uk/newsroom/ourviews/monitor-symptoms-food-diary

My changing body

This website is about voice change for trans people, but it is very clear about the sort of things that can be changed if you want to change the way you speak. It is a good place to start if this applies to you: https://www.asha.org/public/speech/disorders/Voice-and-Communication-Change-for-Transgender-People/

This website has more information about PMS symptoms: https://kidshealth.org/en/teens/menstrual-problems.html

Abusing my body and bad habits

These two websites cover eating disorders:
https://www.rethink.org/advice-and-information/about-mental-illness/learn-more-about-conditions/eating-disorders/
https://www.mind.org.uk/information-support/types-of-mental-health-problems/eating-problems/types-of-eating-disorders/
In the UK only, Childline https://www.childline.org.uk or phone 0800 1111

The physical environment

The best decibel meter app is Decibel X available free for Apple and Android phones.

Further help and guidance

The following people can help you with your voice: the school or college nurse; a doctor; a singing teacher; a speech and drama teacher; a speech and language therapist (SLT). For more specialist help you will need to be referred to an Ear, Nose & Throat (ENT) doctor by your GP. A Laryngologist is the expert in voice problems. You might be treated at a specialist Voice Clinic. Information on a range of topics from vocal health to coping with colds can be found here: https://www.britishvoiceassociation.org.uk/ and here: https://voicefoundation.org/

Photo: Ash Mills

Olivia Sparkhall MA, PGCE is a voice specialist with a particular interest in helping young people to reach their vocal potential. She read for a Masters in Voice Pedagogy and has since had articles published on vocal warm-ups for children, choral music written by women, and composing for the community.

She is a teacher at Godolphin School, Salisbury, UK, where she directs the award-winning Godolphin Vocal Ensemble. In demand as a vocal workshop leader, Olivia has worked with many young choirs, and conducts massed children's choir concerts for the charity, Barnardo's.

An acclaimed composer, Olivia is published by Banks Music Publications, Encore Publications, and Chichester Music Press, as well as being part of the series research and editorial team for the Multitude of Voyces CIC Sacred Music by Women Composers set of anthologies.

Ingram Content Group UK Ltd.
Milton Keynes UK
UKHW052100150523
421784UK00004B/51

9 781909 082717